Presented to the

Juniata College Curriculum Library

By

Raystown Country Reading Council
From
2010-2011 Keystone State Reading Association's
"Keystone to Reading Book Award" List.

ALFRED NOBEL

THE MAN BEHIND THE PEACE PRIZE

The paintings were rendered in oil on canvas
Text Copyright © 2009 Kathy-jo Wargin
Illustration Copyright © 2009 Zachary Pullen

Sleeping Bear Press®

310 North Main Street, Suite 300
Chelsea, MI 48118
www.sleepingbearpress.com

© 2009 Sleeping Bear Press is an imprint of Gale, a part of Cengage Learning.

Printed and bound in China.

First Edition

10 9 8 7 6 5 4 3 2 1

Library of Congress Cataloging-in-Publication Data

Wargin, Kathy-jo.
The man behind the Peace Prize: Alfred Nobel / written by Kathy-jo Wargin;
illustrated by Zachary Pullen.
p. cm.
Summary: "Alfred Nobel was the man who founded what became known as
The Nobel Prizes. Nobel also invented dynamite, becoming very wealthy from
his invention. Saddened by its use for harmful destruction, Nobel left his
fortune to create yearly prizes for those who have rendered the greatest
services to mankind"—Provided by publisher.
ISBN 978-1-58536-281-3
1. Nobel, Alfred Bernhard, 1833-1896—Juvenile literature. 2. Chemical
engineers—Biography—Juvenile literature . 3. Dynamite—Juvenile literature.
4. Nobel Prizes—Juvenile literature. I. Pullen, Zachary, ill. II. Title.
TP268.5.N7W37 2009
660.092—dc22
[B]
2008041297

To all children who carry the vision, the dream, and the willpower to make our world smarter, healthier, safer, and a more peaceful place to live for all people. We need you.

—Kathy-jo

For all the teachers who nurture curiosity.

—Zak

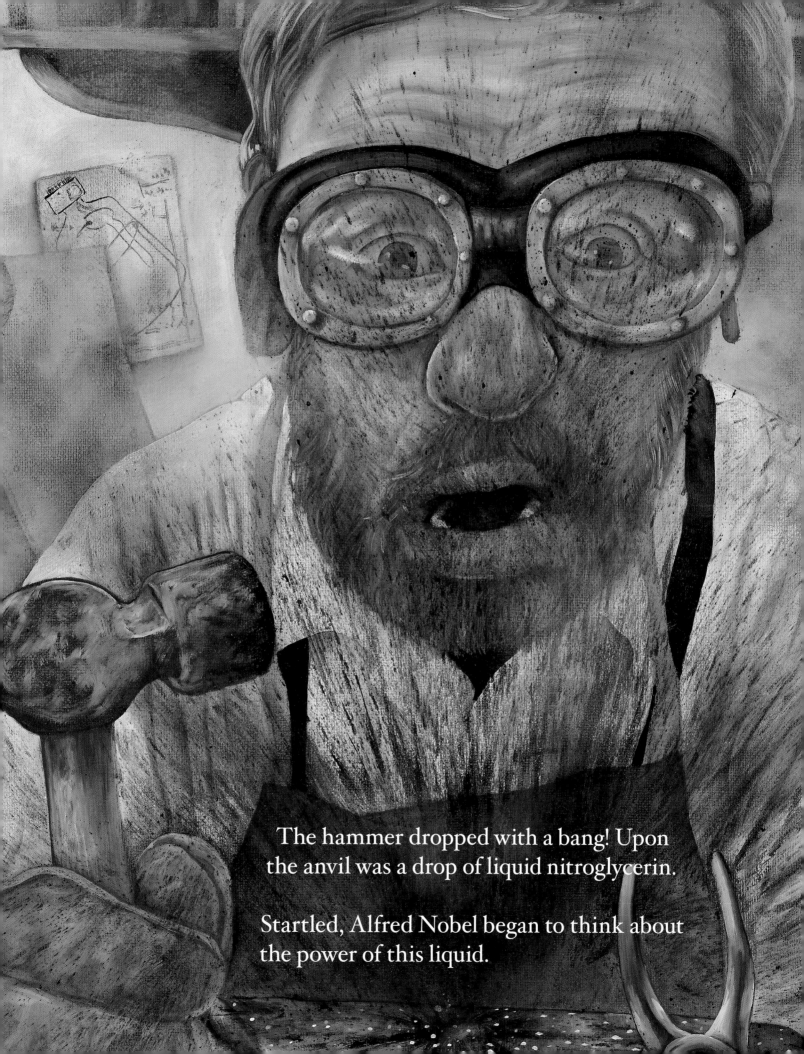

The hammer dropped with a bang! Upon the anvil was a drop of liquid nitroglycerin.

Startled, Alfred Nobel began to think about the power of this liquid.

A liquid like this could cause enough force to blast away rock where bridges and roads and railways needed to be built. It could help militaries have safer weapons. Most often, gunpowder was used for these purposes, but it wasn't very safe. Alfred's love of poetry and literature was equal to his love of science and chemistry. Although he hoped to spend his life as a writer, he soon realized that writing and poetry would have to wait.

Alfred began trying different ways to ignite nitroglycerin safely. With the help of his father and his brothers Robert and Ludvig, he experimented day and night, sometimes mixing the liquid with gunpowder, which made it easier to handle.

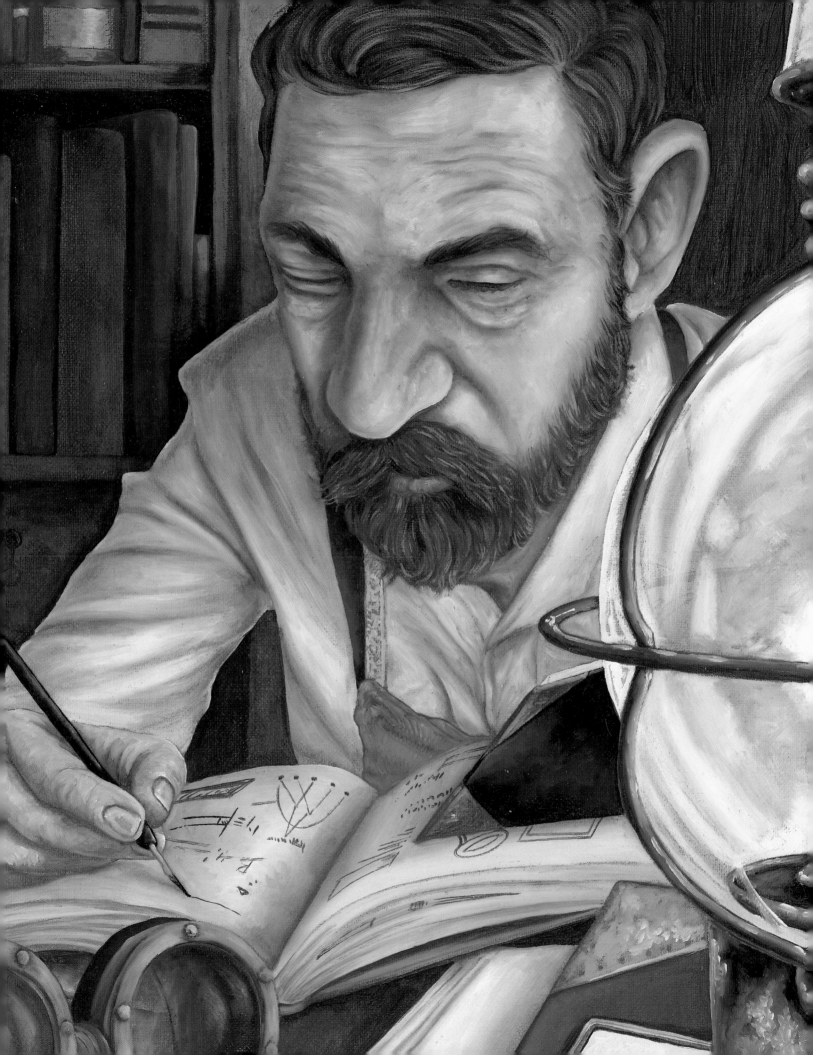

Alfred kept testing until he came up with a wooden plug he could fill with gunpowder. He called the plug a blasting cap. It would help builders ignite the nitroglycerin safely. Alfred was pleased.

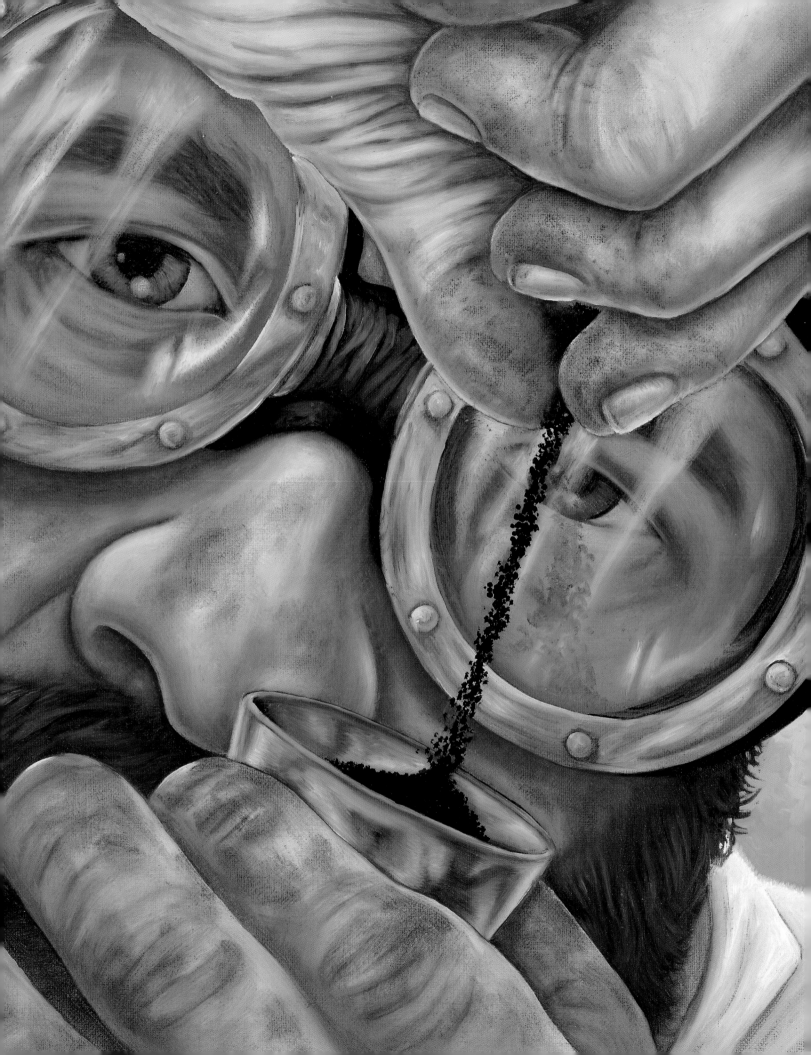

Not long after, Alfred and his brother
Emil began to make and sell nitroglycerin
in their homeland of Sweden. They called
it blasting oil and orders came in from many
places. Just as Alfred hoped, the blasting oil
was used to build roads and railways, bridges,
ports, and towns.

One day in the workshop, Emil and a partner were making some new oil when something went terribly wrong.

BOOM!

Everything exploded, and five people were dead, including Emil.

The tragedy proved one thing to Alfred. He must make nitroglycerin even safer yet. As the pain of his loss troubled him, Alfred worked day and night. Some days he would feel weak and ill, while others he felt lonely and sad, wanting nothing more than to escape into books or poetry.

Two years after Emil died, Alfred mixed nitroglycerin with sand. This made a paste he could roll into the shape of a rod. He realized such rods could be put into holes so builders could make blasts happen only where they wanted. The rods would ignite only if they had a blasting cap, making them unlikely to explode on their own. Finally, Alfred Nobel made nitroglycerin safe to use.

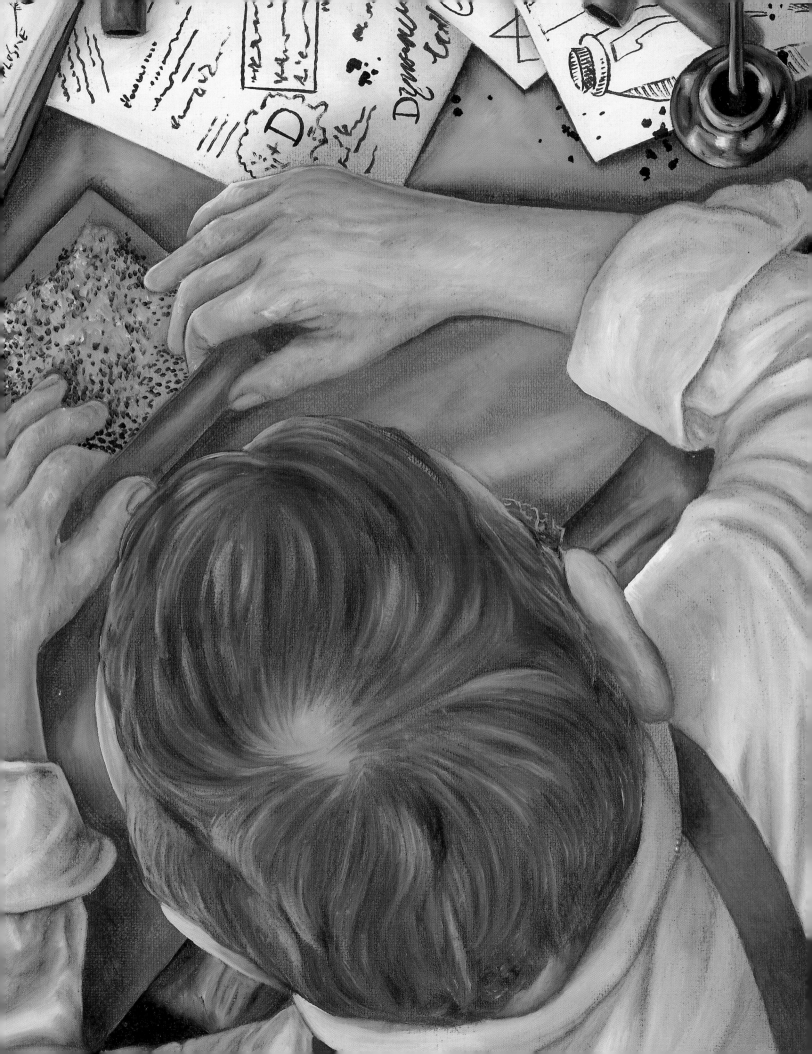

Alfred named his invention after the Greek word *dynamis*, which means power. But to the world, Alfred Nobel had invented something called dynamite.

This made Alfred wealthy and famous. Everybody knew about Alfred Nobel and his dynamite.

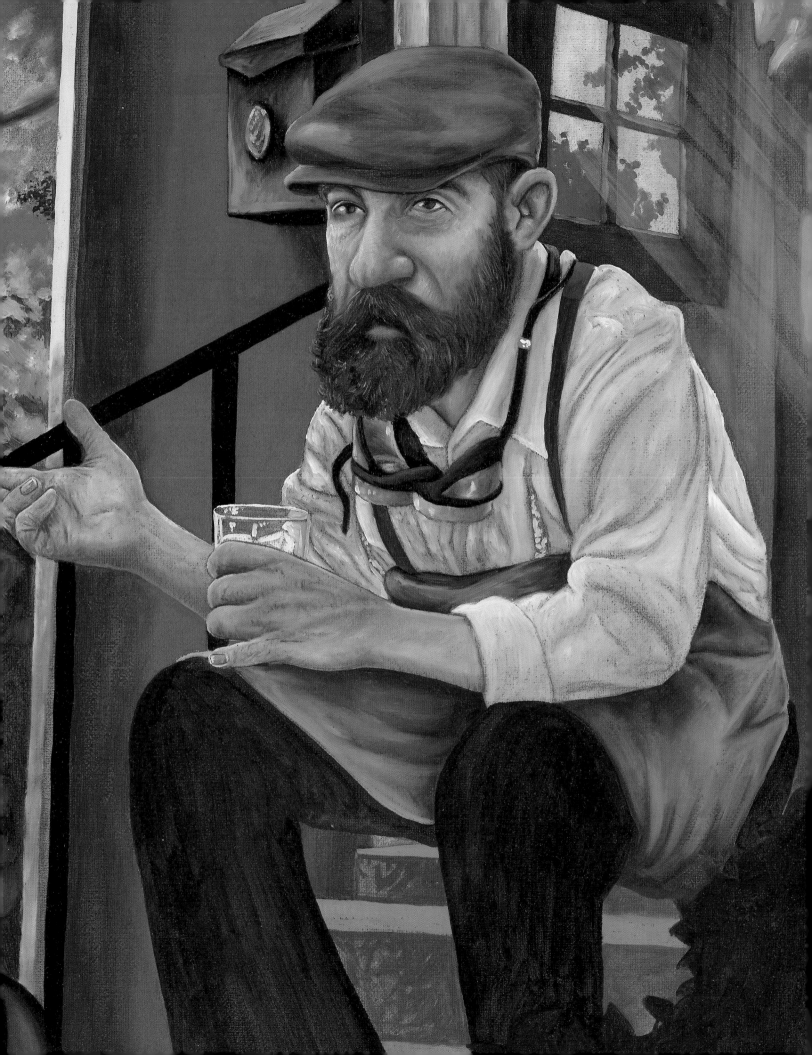

Alfred was happy with his success. Most of all, he hoped his inventions would prevent war. He thought that if people were afraid of the harm that explosions could cause, perhaps they would settle things peacefully first.

But Alfred was wrong.

In many countries, people began to use dynamite to solve problems by hurting others. This made Alfred very sad.

One morning in France, where Alfred was living, people woke to the newspaper headline, "Alfred Nobel is Dead!" It reported that Alfred Nobel, the dynamite king, had died of a heart attack. People everywhere were shocked by the news, but nobody was more shocked than Alfred Nobel.

His brother Ludvig had recently died. The newspaper had reported it wrong.

As Alfred read his own obituary, he realized that others saw him as a man who earned his wealth by inventing ways to injure and kill. For the rest of his days, this made him very sad.

On December 10, 1896, Alfred Nobel died a wealthy but lonely man at his home in Italy. He was buried in Sweden.

His friends and family gathered to hear the reading of his will. After money had been given to a few close friends and relatives, an announcement was made. The entire estate of Alfred Nobel, one of the richest men in all of Europe, would be used to create yearly prizes for those who have rendered the greatest services to humankind.

There would be a prize for accomplishment in physics; another for chemical discovery or improvement; a prize for physiology or medicine; and a prize for literature.

And last was to be a special prize. It would be for peace.

So on that very day, Alfred Nobel, the man who loved literature and poetry and the art of discovery, left a legacy to be remembered for always—as the man who founded what became known throughout the world as The Nobel Prizes.

THE NOBEL PEACE PRIZE WINNERS

The Nobel Peace Prize has been awarded to individuals or organizations since 1901. For years not listed on the following chart, no prize was awarded. To learn more about Alfred Nobel and the Nobel Prizes, visit Nobelprize.org.

2008 MARTTI AHTISAARI

2007 *Intergovernmental Panel on Climate Change*, AL GORE

2006 MUHAMMAD YUNUS, *Grameen Bank*

2005 *International Atomic Energy Agency*, MOHAMED ELBARADEI

2004 WANGARI MAATHAI

2003 SHIRIN EBADI

2002 JIMMY CARTER

2001 *United Nations*, KOFI ANNAN

2000 KIM DAE-JUNG

1999 MÉDECINS SANS FRONTIÈRES

1998 JOHN HUME, DAVID TRIMBLE

1997 *International Campaign to Ban Landmines*, JODY WILLIAMS

1996 CARLOS FILIPE XIMENES BELO, JOSÉ RAMOS-HORTA

1995 JOSEPH ROTBLAT, *Pugwash Conferences on Science and World Affairs*

1994 YASSER ARAFAT, SHIMON PERES, YITZHAK RABIN

1993 NELSON MANDELA, F.W. DE KLERK

1992 RIGOBERTA MENCHÚ TUM

1991 AUNG SAN SUU KYI

1990 MIKHAIL GORBACHEV

1989 THE 14TH DALAI LAMA

1988 *United Nations Peacekeeping Forces*

1987 OSCAR ARIAS SÁNCHEZ

1986 ELIE WIESEL

1985 *International Physicians for the Prevention of Nuclear War*

1984 DESMOND TUTU

1983 LECH WALESA

1982 ALVA MYRDAL, ALFONSO GARCÍA ROBLES

1981 *Office of the United Nations High Commissioner for Refugees*

1980 ADOLFO PÉREZ ESQUIVEL

1979 MOTHER TERESA

1978 ANWAR al-SADAT, MENACHEM BEGIN

1977 *Amnesty International*

1976 BETTY WILLIAMS, MAIREAD CORRIGAN

1975 ANDREI SAKHAROV

1974 SEÁN MacBRIDE, EISAKU SATO

1973 HENRY KISSINGER, LE DUC THO

1971 WILLY BRANDT	1933 SIR NORMAN ANGELL
1970 NORMAN BORLAUG	1931 JANE ADDAMS, NICHOLAS MURRAY BUTLER
1969 *International Labour Organization*	1930 NATHAN SÖDERBLOM
1968 RENÉ CASSIN	1929 FRANK B. KELLOGG
1965 *United Nations Children's Fund*	1927 FERDINAND BUISSON, LUDWIG QUIDDE
1964 MARTIN LUTHER KING JR.	1926 ARISTIDE BRIAND, GUSTAV STRESEMANN
1963 *International Committee of the Red Cross, League of Red Cross Societies*	1925 SIR AUSTEN CHAMBERLAIN, CHARLES G. DAWES
1962 LINUS PAULING	1922 FRIDTJOF NANSEN
1961 DAG HAMMARSKJÖLD	1921 HJALMAR BRANTING, CHRISTIAN LANGE
1960 ALBERT LUTULI	1920 LÉON BOURGEOIS
1959 PHILIP NOEL-BAKER	1919 WOODROW WILSON
1958 GEORGES PIRE	1917 *International Committee of the Red Cross*
1957 LESTER BOWLES PEARSON	1913 HENRI LA FONTAINE
1954 *Office of the United Nations High Commissioner for Refugees*	1912 ELIHU ROOT
1953 GEORGE C. MARSHALL	1911 TOBIAS ASSER, ALFRED FRIED
1952 ALBERT SCHWEITZER	1910 *Permanent International Peace Bureau*
1951 LÉON JOUHAUX	1909 AUGUSTE BEERNAERT, PAUL HENRI D'ESTOURNELLES DE CONSTANT
1950 RALPH BUNCHE	1908 KLAS PONTUS ARNOLDSON, FREDRIK BAJER
1949 LORD BOYD ORR	1907 ERNESTO TEODORO MONETA, LOUIS RENAULT
1947 *Friends Service Council, American Friends Service Committee*	1906 THEODORE ROOSEVELT
1946 EMILY GREENE BALCH, JOHN R. MOTT	1905 BERTHA VON SUTTNER
1945 CORDELL HULL	1904 *Institute of International Law*
1944 *International Committee of the Red Cross*	1903 RANDAL CREMER
1938 *Nansen International Office for Refugees*	1902 ÉLIE DUCOMMUN, ALBERT GOBAT
1937 ROBERT CECIL	1901 HENRY DUNANT, FRÉDÉRIC PASSY
1936 CARLOS SAAVEDRA LAMAS	
1935 CARL VON OSSIETZKY	
1934 ARTHUR HENDERSON	

KATHY-JO WARGIN

Kathy-jo Wargin is the best-selling author of more than 30 books for children. Among her many awards for her work are an International Reading Association (IRA) Children's Choice Award for *The Legend of the Loon* and an IRA Teacher's Choice Award for *Win One for the Gipper*. Kathy-jo lives in Minnesota.

ZACHARY PULLEN

Zachary Pullen's picture-book illustrations have won awards and garnered starred reviews. He has been honored several times with acceptance into the prestigious Society of Illustrators juried shows and *Communication Arts Illustration Annual* of the best in current illustration. Zak lives in Wyoming with his wife and son.

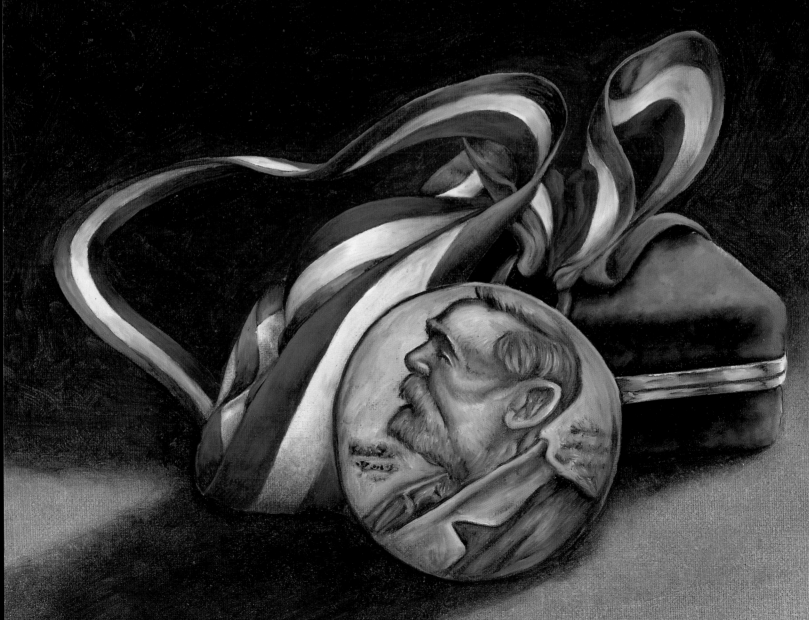